CW00406100

STARBORN BOOKS

Also by Peter Naumann

WINTER COUNT

Peter Naumann

HOLM

For Laura

Peter Naumann

STARBORN BOOKS

HOLM
Peter Naumann

First published in June 2016
by Starborn Books
Cardiff and Nuremberg

E-mail: sales@starbornbooks.co.uk
Website: www.starbornbooks.co.uk

Cover painting by Anuk Naumann

ISBN 978 1 899530 50 2

ACKNOWLEDGEMENTS

So many people have contributed something – however obliquely – to this book, and in ways that cannot easily be acknowledged here, that here I will simply say thank you to everyone who has provided me with support, encouragement, and stimulation over the past three years; God willing, and given time, I can thank them all in person.

Space permits a few specific acknowledgements, however – first and foremost, as ever, to Peter Oram – friend, editor, and advocate, without whom *Holm* would not exist (or not yet, anyway). Charlie Sharp once again joined forces with Peter in winnowing chaff from the manuscript, as did my comrade Michael Malay. If I have not necessarily followed their advice in every instance, I have always appreciated it.

Gudrun Oram took on the tedious task of ironing out syntactical irregularities; the book as it stands therefore owes an enormous amount to her. Once again Anuk Naumann (or mum, as I usually call her) has supplied a painting which I hope will make everyone judge this book by its cover.

My thanks also go to Josh Adcock, Anna Godfrey, Samatar Elmi, Millie Morris, Jenny Messenger, and to all my fellow participants in the workshop run by Rachael Boast as Bristol University's poet in residence in 2013, for their criticism and support; Steven Lovatt, Miriam Guastalla, and Ed Davis are among those who have seen and commented on versions of these poems in their infancy, while conversations in person and on paper with Mo Browne, Michael Agathangelou, Tom Farshi, Meg Wiessner, Irene Espinosa, Emily Hopfinger, Clare Carlile, Robert Beavis, Anna Pearson, and of course Holly Harrington, have opened rich seams of insight and set many a spark to the dry tinder. Support and encouragement has come from many quarters, but my family, and the extended family provided by the Multifaith Chaplaincy at Bristol University and the OxGrow community gardening project, each of them a foretaste of the socialist paradise for which we keep our fingers crossed, have been of special importance. My apologies to Rustem Rustem for not taking his advice and writing about Genghis Khan (yet), but my thanks for the tip (and watch this space...)

This book is dedicated to Ella and to Liz, who as I write this continue to make Leeds a better and happier place, much as they did to Bristol; I cannot thank either of them enough.

Peter Naumann, Great Rollright, Winter 2015/6

'Urraca', 'Lonely Planet', & 'Landfall', have previously appeared in *Cadaverine* magazine (online); 'Imlac' has previously been displayed on the website of the Bristol Poetry Institute.

I

SKIN AND WHISPERS

Branching Out

Take to the trees and speak

with any that return

the compliment; forbear

toward those with their tongues

still tethered to the root, or fingers

choking any chance of music from the flute.

Take only what the air can

give, what water,

earth and fire cannot keep; accept

each limb that bears you

up, and never compromise

with solid ground. Uncertainties,

of course, abound, so,

faced with gallows,

ladders, cranes and crows'

nests, main and mizzen masts, make up

your mind as you see

fit, for doubtless it is just

as well to scatter some

discrepancies and lapses after you,

leaving your apologists a little work to do.

Under the Weather

Rain, continual and grey and now and then

loud as city centre

traffic on the roofs of Redland,

darkens the wooden and worn metal

parts of railway lines, cajoling

ravens into sycamores, magpies

to explore the pros and cons of ash

leaves against willowherb or oleander.

All morning sun, all evening

breeze and troubled

stars and jackets with the bronze

rubbed from their zippers'

teeth, the denim sparse

as arctic woodland at the elbows.

~

You see nothing, you see

steel or ivy and the spilt,

split pouches where horse

chestnuts put their luxuries

to sleep for summer,

swallowed

by the light we call September.

~

Days like this, you turn

away from metalled

roads, down gravel

tracks where work has stopped,

the plastic and the cables

visible, the hats and tabards stacked

in cairns - fluorescent heaps

to comfort any passing

seraph pining for the palette of the sun,

the trinkets of the happy

south and resins of the coastal ranges.

~

Now the rains have come

once more, I will climb

the worn stairs and the weary

ladders to the unroofed

chamber in the western gallery,

to hear the song that water

makes on canvas

noon and night and morning.

Postcard from the Trust Territory

Lagoons and mangrove, mountains

rising in surprising, tidy

rings, and somewhere, hidden

by the whims of sun and cloud

on water, the Lapita

coins and crumbs of earthenware,

jettisoned ordnance, anchors,

Japanese and American

shirts and shoes and ration tins.

~

Less than a hundred

yards to my right,

inside an ark of stippled glass,

the oldest inch of rock

found on Earth so far

reclines on felt, while straight

ahead of me, a dinosaur in rainy

steel watches the wet mountain

bikes, saloons, and hatchbacks

westering, the first and second

year students eye each

other for as long as lights

stay red, then cross the dark

road and disperse, some

for their books and some their beds.

Lonely Planet

Buildings begin to lose

hold of corners and conclusions

this side of November

and the narrow river. None

will help me, none point

out the bridge or stair

except a star not yet

abroad nor yellow and still

wary of leading

witnesses in any silver stint of sky.

Amedeo

for Charlie

You did not, perhaps

you could not, live

at La Ruche, where refugees

from ghetto and Okhrana

gathered, only dreaming

of such a poverty before,

nor at the Bateau

Lavoir,

until much later; instead,

you sought out

Brancuşi (who had walked

across the Carpathians, and was known

to serve sumptuous meals

from the oven and the oilpress he had built

himself), composed

19

voluminous

letters of thanks and admiration

to the principal chiefs of Africa - never

                      to write nor send them - sat

in 1908 under your black

umbrella with Akhmatova,

reciting

Verlaine in turn between

incessant rhymes of summer

                                  rain, and painted

her as Queen of Cush and Nubia and both Egypts.

After hours you carved whatever

wood the city could afford - your caryatids

the exact

length of sleepers

cleared from the Métro Barbès-

Rochechouart, heads

waking out of stolen

stone, cut with as little

noise as possible

once the quarrymen had downed

their chisels for the night.

       War came, and stone

became too scarce,

too costly;

       later you would mourn

the loss of stone

as the great wound,

still open and dividing

your first life from what followed.

Oppen's Razor

for Mike

You puzzle an inch of heart,

query the lathe, appreciate

the point, the lyric

        and laconic

purpose of the mode produced –

clarity, always

        clarity, attempted

in each fraction and inflection,

words and things no sooner

noticed than attended –

          in passing

through your hands they come

clean and break

free, go

     wild, taciturn and mended.

Midrash

Melon on the housetop
has two choices
(Merwin, from the Chinese)

A fork in the high road and a whole

dresser's trove of cutlery above

us – satellites and saucers

neat as knives and spoons, stars

giving dawn the slip and glass the wink.

Is this the true path, dipping

between the bright

water and the stacks of hay?

Did I hear you

right when you said that

a pumpkin

in the rafters could go either way?

Sans Souci

To think of trees is treason (Brecht)

Funny how things change (Mark Cocker)

You have to talk to trees, but how

would you address the first

you ever meet?

Lime, perhaps, considering it

wise to keep a little acid

back to whet your tongue, but, faced

with such exuberant and unkempt

beauty - the *Marie-*

Celeste, laundry frayed to cobweb

whickering from each rope, as frigate

birds and shearwaters play

their games of chance

between the holystones and fenders –

just try and stop

yourself from crying *linden, linden, linden*

II

HINTERLAND

New Cut

Riding, thinking how to break

a poem for you and about you,

I scared three

pigeons from the barley - one

almost into my wheels -

hauling on short

wings and shallow

lungs against the burning,

blond high summer

air, making for the ash

stands, hawthorns, and hidden

lodges on the far side of the field.

Bats had been as sudden, feinting

as they gained and lost

their quarry in a shape

you might have drawn from

memory but never

once expected to describe such

loops above the tidal river, each

commotion of fur and ultrasound as tidy,

tight and legible as glyphs

devised by Noah to remind

himself who occupied those nesting

boxes nailed among the rafters of the ark.

~

For more than two months you had taught me

how to read the tide and harbour, how

to spell the city's secret

name in water and anticipate

now prodigal, now meagre

measures, which stretches

have been housed, however

soon they may cut

short their stay, and which still

run without a rein or bridle and will answer

any goddess with the moon's voice

when she bids them

leave their beds and follow her

song out, below the hammered

fret and strum of road and rail

bridges, beyond abandoned

warehouses and windmills, smelting

grounds and smokestacks to the start of the grey

                              sea. And here,

although the clouds gave little

hint of parting, nor the heavens'

screed of rolling

to the corners of the sky, and vision

remained as free and rare and fugitive

as before, there was another

lesson painted on the wall, for anyone

to see, who came,

as we had, to the river's brim, to drink:

                    dishevelled, happy

creatures teeming, stretching cramped

sea legs, unfurling

trunks and straitening

the knotted coils of bodies cooped

up forty days and forty

nights inside a tub of pitch and gopher

wood, all whoops and hollers

to see earth again,

trumpeting

as they ran

after the flood, into the bone dry garden.

Landfall

Winter as now, when last

I read

your tally of the islands –

                  scarcity

of water, plethora of sand

~

        as though summer

had no say

on this score,

your words have kept

their shape, the ocean hers

Urraca

Between the brick and timber

houses you find trees and tilt

your tail, a new sword,

nod your head and take

the nearest crop, the tithe

paid by bakers'

wives and butchers'

daughters to the goddess

who delights in thrift and larceny,

collecting squandered fruit as fallen coin

Imlac

        Bells at odds in the town

below, each flight

reiterating ever so

slightly

inconsistent

exegeses of the tropic

        night, he led

me to a chamber in the north

keep, up six hundred

steps, where the derelict flying

machines of the eighteenth

century were stored –

        silk, nickel

wire and balsa wood,

wings, tails and pedals warped

with too much winter

        light and summer rain.

'Take whatever serviceable

        gear may remain,'

he said. 'For me

these relics serve a moral,

rather than an aeronautic purpose.'

Scenes from the Little Ice Age

i.   Rouen

I remember standing a long time, shivering

in rain as one of those

ghosts or Europeans spoke

toward me - at me,

maybe, or about me. I remember

the noise and smell and inconsistent

colours of the rain

on that side of the cold

grey water, and that grey man's voice,

his beard and his tidy, complicated clothes.

ii.   Galveston

First of all, don't tell me

what I did and what

I did not see,

                    whether

land or water left

these marks all over me.

My bones and nightmares bear

witness to an unknown

country's snubs and greetings,

my skin has changed

since this continent, these sands

began

writing prayers and edicts

on my heart and my two hands.

~

Between Sanlúcar

      de Barrameda and Lake Texcoco

the trees speak every dialect but mine.

When you plant a nopal

      or a cocoa palm, draw a line

in the earth, between that blind tongue

sounding

out the springs of peace

in shale and loam and stubborn

clay, and the surface, where each

morning breaks another

treaty, and the wars for sunlight never cease.

iii.   Arafura

Remember seven of us running

through a dream, a dry land.

Between the field of spelt and water

tower, where a gulley waits

another season on the overdue

return of hungry river

ghosts, we paused, pricked every

ear for the hue and cry and panting

pack, and caught

our breath as deer leapt the intervals ahead.

iv.   Jumala

In stone or ivory, you were a bird, a fish,

a butterfly, mother of the many horses.

Your arms were raised, a sickle

moon in one hand and your eye

open forever. In the Urals,

devotees brought gold,

hung what they could

garner in the branches of your grove,

so you could have a brilliant new skin,

like the snake discarding her brown

habit for a year of copper and electrum.

In Tyumen, the old hunter told

treasure-seekers that the golden

woman was no longer to be found;

she had been taken up, away

from the sight and reach of men,

away from the dust of steppe and city,

the laughing sun, and the creatures that forget.

Orpah

You had the deep waters, and now stones

in any wall on your side

teem with shells and shapes of fishes.

We had the shallow reaches, and the sands

still run between our fingers to the river.

We have watched them cutting

fruit trees with bronze axes, knives, and diesel-

driven saws, until the slopes, no longer

flummoxed by roots, come

shivering down to silt the wells and washing-pools.

Loess is your gift, as always; blithe as dry

winds from the north, you waived

all purchase on far places, heap

these stones and arguments with dust

until we cannot sweep away or reason out

their patina, their derivations. Only

trace and tendency

remain – pits, gullies and condemned

paths eking a memory of thirst and anger

slaked where salt augments a caustic surplus.

Morning in the Medical Library

Clouds stay where they were

an hour before, as tiles,

buds and branches analyse

inflections of sunlight, minor

clauses in the air. Bristol is not yet

sure which century it has woken

into, whether sails or funnels

will throng the Avon come high tide,

what confidence to place in the potato

harvest or the price of wine, if sugar still

reeks of iron and broken

skin, what price strong human

bone and labour fetches

on the open market, and how many

votes it takes to build a new Jerusalem,

or bribes to keep the bricks and mortar

under lock and key. With my left hand

I pull segment after orange

segment from the fruit held in my right,

waiting for the individual

streets and railings, hawthorn

brakes and hungry ghosts to come in sight.

Messenger

Daughter of the winter moon, you had us all

hoodwinked, knew

never a blade descends from gaudy hilts

such as the bandits stash into their breeches,

lying in wait beside the moorland road

between the new capital and the holy, ruined city.

Just so, you saw through every load of silver

carp or ragged money, and regarded

trees up to their toes in ice as steady

comrades, however few their contributions

to the common fund, however rare

their greetings, and however cold their gaze.

~

As March gets wind of gold, keep fast

that memory of me - green

coat and laughter in the later rains, as I

keep thumbing a thin but stubborn string,

turning from the chill

instalments of another winter, coaxing

promises of resurrection and the spring,

already thrilled by grace

notes and near harmonies of summer.

Namesake

Simon,

Simeon – a glance will

find you everywhere

in scripture, raising

your voice in prophecy,

your right arm in anger, kneeling

by the bed of Jacob to be

blessed and reprimanded, sleeping

between two soldiers (for the last

time, as you thought, until that

kid without

a hair on his face turned

the key and took you out

into the empty street), running

for Rhoda and a friendly house,

expecting, every moment, morning

to find you and your wardens,

unshaven and unrested, arm in brawny arm.

~

Another evening darkens, without moon. Tomorrow

it will be August, and harder still

to talk of living in high summer, from the fat of the land.

Another bright and rainless day gone begging, thinking

the right thoughts and doing

nothing with them, combing aubergine and walnut

leaves for symptoms of the kingdom or the coming

trial. None will be granted, do you not

remember, not even a gourd's shade or a dry wind,

let alone a young man running from the potager,

the last of his linen cast

behind him with the swords and torches, severed

ears, and every blithe or bitter Sabbath

word exchanged as barley

flushed and shuddered, an ocean courted by the sun.

~

Perhaps you forgot it all – each

admonition and rebuke,

each fish, each city

contrary to your demands, each time

morning found you

beside ashes in the servant's

quarters – when you saw him, same

as ever, and hardly a scratch

on him at that distance, calling

from the shingle, and before

you knew a thing

about it, grey salt water was a yard

above you and the Lord alone

knows how many below,

while the voice kept sounding, and you swam.

Passage

After the utmost, uppermost

shining slope of Earth,

watching

Venus perfect as a penny

eke a path

across the sun through tinfoil,

losing one rim's

certainty and finding

another quite herself again,

we tried our hands at wind and water -

first lowered as far as the system

allows, then keeping

every eye on board

skinned for a clew of silver deep

enough to float all seven

tonnes of us right out of Wales,

toward the green buoys, yellow

cardinals, dilapidated

lights and campfires

and at last the Avon, hiding

between mudflats, marram,

dotterels and stints,

a slender dab among a slew of glints.

Exegesis

We all took you for an expert, a safe pair of hands.

How our faces fell

when you mistook the mistletoe

for a snagged balloon, laboured your translation

from the magpie's codex, and stood as if

you were blind before the trace of moonlight in the sands.

Perhaps you had been lucky, when you led us dancing

through the slim lanes and gaps

in the city's armour as the sun looked on. Perhaps

the lightning's touch had not worn off

by then, or the thunder stopped

rolling through your ears, an Atlantic chancing

everything on this throw of the tide. We had braided

ragwort and campion into our hair, stitched

paper stars and the dry, curry-scented seed

pods of alexanders to our shirts. Now we seemed more

ready for sacrifice or surrender than such revels.

Turning from the cryptic, unforgiving shore, you waded

out into the river, to the green seal-haunted rock.

There you waited, grey eyes fixed downstream,

where the water swerves away. At any moment

we expected the river goddess, with her train, to rise

from the gravel, take you to a secret harbour

beyond our wit to find, and bury the lone key to the lock.

III

GHOST ROAD

Daguerrotype

                              In studio photographs, baseball

heroes of the nineteenth

century strike poses

straight from the walls of the Uffizi:

                              a renaissance

prince, with the pale globe poised

between his thumb and index

finger like a fresh Murano

glass or Aztec doll, his retinue

looking on with approval from outside

the frame, awaiting

their smatter of munificence;

                              an hidalgo, slouched

against split pillars

while a village burns, the undesirables

baptised or bundled

into boats, his scabbard

scuffing conquered ground;

                        a harvester, all but the last

sheaf in, scooping a pebble

from the furrow, arm

crooked to sling

a perfect strike across the gleaned and gathered barley field.

Meridian

i.

Mild days in February, milder

yet come March, and shingles

speak of nought but cinders,

sunlight, and the fall of cities,

as first indigo, then amethyst

breaks ground below the fort.

~

Abandoned by the moon and salt,

each mouth in water frames

a saw, an adage or an iron

simile to test the ring as pewter

falls upon the mountains, fool's

gold and bdellium on the plain.

~

Always standing just to this

side of the real world and always

left behind, leave walking

for another lesson, learn

to sing today and run

tomorrow as you always wanted.

ii.

Say nothing more without

your share of loess,

rain or risen

water - without

the silts and freshets of the Rosebud,

Little Bighorn,

Powder, or Missouri in your mouth.

There will be words enough to follow,

welcome, and resist –

as spotted cattle, past

all counting, keep on coming

through shallows near

the camp the Cheyenne,

Crow, and Mandan,

as much as the Lakota, know

as the site of much game and many caches.

iii.

Near White River, one road

goes to Rosebud,

the other to Parmelee. There

my great-grandfather led a Ghost

Dance. The hoop is still there –

on a good summer

day you can still make it out.

An old man – Black Bear was his name –

fell into a vision world there, and lay

on the ground as the others danced.

After a time he rose

to his feet, facing north with arms

outstretched. In plain daylight

the people saw a little

flash of lightning in his hand, just

like a looking glass. When he had been

smoked and fanned with sweet grass,

a piece of rock was seen

in his hand – no rock

you'd ever see on Earth. Moon rock,

you see – and the dancers came

out of their trances with food in their hands,

the flesh of moons and stars.

The smell of sweet, burning

grass still lingers there.

iv.

My father taught me how to ride

all kinds of horses – yellow,

white, and mottled.

I never used a saddle. Then

Dad showed me how

to handle hammer, wedge, and saw.

Beat going to school, any day.

Between seven and fourteen I learned

dancing from a medicine man –

the hoop dance, the gourd dance,

the eagle dance and the rope dance.

They are sacred ceremonies, prayers.

By the time I was nine I could dance

with five hoops, all whirling,

to the beat of my brother's

drum, and soon I danced with seven.

Eleven years old and dancing, I heard

the spirit talk to me, like two stones

clicking, and the whistle of a bird.`

I was always learning – the eagle hoop,

chair hoop and lightning hoop. When I was twelve,

I danced with sixteen hoops – and twenty-one

two years later. It was then it happened - a teenager

at the big powwow, fixing up my costume,

and a cloud comes down; the voice of a bird

tells me 'Hokshila, this is the moment and the place'.

That day I danced as never before, and danced

my last. Afterwards I hung up the hoops of the boy

I had been.

As well as the hoops, I would dance with the gourd,

with a spirit talking in it.

Shaking the gourd, the spirits

talked to me in small, encouraging, ghostly voices.

v.

Crow Dog and the other Lakota say

you came

down from the moon

across a bridge of lightning.

Now you walk the desert road,

eyes fastened on the iron mountain,

hands spilling dust and hair

dishevelled by a cold and quenchless fire.

vi.

To make it right, start looking

for the proper sort of rocks;

you find them

on the prairie and the hills. They are earth

hardened into stone,

solid, dull and durable, without sparkle or sheen.

Examine them and you will see

faint designs, green tracings –

ancient colonies of moss losing their grip

after sun and ice have been on at them

for a thousand winters. Some think

birds traced these patterns. You can see

your future in them. An old man

once told me he could see

a river and a ruined bridge,

waters overflowing, floods on their way.

Go down to the creek and cut

twelve white willow trees.

Peel and plant them

in a circle in the ground.

These form the skeleton of the hut.

They are the bones of our people.

The sweat house is small. It is the universe;

every living spirit is inside. In the centre

we scoop a circular hole. The dark

stones from hill and prairie will be placed

in here later. We pray

to Wakan Tanka, to the Great Spirit, as we do this.

The power of the Great Spirit will be there. It will

become the heart and navel of the whole world.

The entrance to the lodge faces the west, the dying sun.

Don't believe the anthropologists when they write

that lodges always face the east – those are the heyoka

lodges, lodges of clowns who do everything different,

everything the other way around from everybody else.

Before the entrance to the lodge we plant two

forked sticks, and place a third

horizontally across, to make a rack for the sacred pipe.

Some people would put a buffalo skùll there,

with six offerings of tobacco tied to the horns.

Others put a black-and-white stick there.

standing for day and night.

A pail of water is kept handy. This is the water of life, and must be

drawn from a fresh and running stream. In former days,

we filled a skin bag with water, but

the old decorated bags are gone now.

An ordinary pail must do.

Witness

Back from Malaya, the rededication

ceremonies of the south migrate

a little further with each passing

hour from memory to many words

which marry well and never will

divorce from reams of paper

put aside for pulp or burning.

~

                              Perhaps

you ate the dwindling rice and dug, like

all the rest, for pine roots, for anything

to fuel the Zeroes, the remaining ships.

All spring and summer, engines

overhead, trailing

steam like snow beneath toboggan

runners, each plane no bigger

than a matchbox, easy

enough to hide by palm or fist

held up against the blue;

                    all spring

and summer pages cluttering

the camphor trees and sluices, littering

Aio-bashi -

                    Springtime

in March and April. The cherry

blossom season. But July

and August will be the season of ashes

~

You had grown familiar

with the sound of aircraft, expecting

propaganda, and didn't

get excited by so few,

nor by the parachute, the dawdle

timed to let the pilots put sufficient air

miles behind them and their crews,

between the thirty-

       seven of them in their dark

glasses and the designated city

by the ocean in the south,

each second

escaping

further from the morning and the ashes

Painted Chamber

Last night I dreamed a yellow biplane, circa 1924,

executed barrel rolls and looped the loop

above the dachas, sunflowers, and fields of sorghum.

When the engine fumed and sputtered, streaming

smoke and cinders, and a scream of fire

followed the plunging tail behind a grassy ridge,

the farmhands and the film crew from Penza ran

up the slope, to the crater's lip – but the reel

cut before the body count began, and there

we were in the plastered chamber,

going about it the same old way,

tentative and tipsy, in bashful hints and sallies,

quenching and refreshing the reluctant light

until creatures accustomed to soft breezes and bright

sunshine stood about,

their breath and language laboured in the garb of night.

Medicine Wheel

Hide your hair and your history,

your teeth and nails,

the scar on your shoulder and the umber

birthmark in the shape of Lake Itasca on your breast;

you can hide in the steppes and sand hills of the west,

in the dark forest, by the inland sea,

but you cannot hide

your heart or your white-hot soul from me.

~

In Byzantine purple – the shade you wore

when I met you waiting on the station

steps as rain

began to raise the river and the flotsam

around Isis Lock – I underline

passages from Leonard Crow Dog's

rendition of the sweat lodge and the vision quest:

how his father told him that

the moon had gathered all the waters

from a tiny drop; how the red pipe

stone from the sacred quarry in the Santee country

was the flesh of the real wild human

beings, and the smoke that passed

through was the breath of Tunkashila,

grandfather and creator of each living thing;

how with the help of Good Lance and Arrow Sight

he had endured the scalding steam, spoken

at each lifting of the door, walked

barefoot up the hill to the stand of pine and cedar

where coyotes sang their moon songs, planted

the four flags and gone

down into the pit, to cry for a dream

with forty patches

cut from his mother's forearm,

the pipe, the eagle tail,

deer tail and spider altar; how Reuben

Red Feather came to him, who had been

killed in the war, as did a woodpecker,

gopher, and a lightning bug, and he had come

out after four days and four nights and eaten

corn again and knew

he was reborn, committed

to the spirit and his people,

the *ikche wichasha*, with many

quests and visions yet to come.

~

Tongue between his lips, our friend had drawn

a path around the harbour,

around the towers and the boats,

to the green parts of the city and the roads

back to his door. I walked

toward the Øresund, past spars and sails,

wondering if it was appropriate to tell

you all about them, and should

have, wise or otherwise, through thickets,

over slopes of grass and gravel,

past sandlots, glimpsing lithe and happy games,

to the formal gardens and domesticated

channels, sitting against logs and earthworks,

reading the *agrapha* and returning,

remembering, as I watched

leaves trail into the lazy current,

how we lay once among the willow

tendrils and the flowering balsam,

that day we rowed back, over burnished waters,

after almost reaching a rapprochement

between rivers once single and long since

estranged.

Above the gateway to the mosque at Fatehpur

Sikri, Akbar had instructed

masons to carve

words attributed to Jesus, enjoining all

who entered there to build

themselves no dwelling on the earth,

but rather pass

over this world as one would cross a bridge.

It has been written that

there were no bridges in Palestine

when Jesus worked and wandered

from Galilee to Emmaus, though Mark records

a journey to Phoenicia, where the Son of Man,

with fishermen and bandits and holy,

shameless women by his side might

just have seen the great mole

on the coast at Tyre, and walked upon it,

between crowded and exploited waters.

Apocrypha

surveyed and daydreams flickering,

I left Malmohuset and crossed

a busy road back

into the residential areas,

remembering to look

the other way for traffic. weighing

merits of alternate titles

for a book of poems hardly underway,

following the faded line my friend had

traced, I began to lose my way, but

turned into Holmgatan, children

milling round the bright

plastic bins with ice

creams, and could

see that I was almost there at last.

Wasf

        Rise with the riddled

mulberry leaves, oak

        gall and magpie feathers

clinging to your hair,

                your dress

the colour of sequoia bark

after an evening's dose of rain;

                go, but tell me

first what the sun's

                thirst or the moon's

long hunger holds

                for mountain grass,

what injury the wind

                may wreak or have

repaired before we lie once more,

as one against the summer's grain.

Kidron

Perhaps in the walled city, beyond

fields of flax we took for standing

water, beets and maize where quails

hide whenever a hawk or engine starts

up from the shadows - perhaps

there, under the medlars and the mulberries,

trestles are still laid with snakeroot, dandelion,

pepperwort and chicory, the bright

leaves, spice and vinegar demanded

by the high feast, oil and olives

from the north, the pulses and the sycamore's

issue, enough to sustain

an honoured teacher or a holy fool

through a hundred warnings and a week of dust.

NOTES

[Branching Out]

The poem draws – rather loosely – on Italo Calvino's wonderful novella *The Baron in the Trees* (*Il barone rampante*).

[Amedeo]

Details of Modigliani's life in Paris before the First World War come predominantly from Carol Mann, *Modigliani* (Thames & Hudson, 1980).

[Midrash]

Midrash is traditional Rabbinic scriptural interpretation, as found in the Talmuds and many associated writings of the first millennium CE; the aphorism translated by W.S. Merwin can be found among many other equally pithy 'Chinese figures' in his collection *East Window: The Asian Translations* (Copper Canyon Press, 1998), p. 136.

[*Sans Souci*]

The quote from Brecht, and Mark Cocker's response, come from Cocker's, *Claxton: Field Notes from a Small Planet* (Jonathan Cape, 2014), p. 81).

[*Urraca*]

Urraca – a name borne by mediaeval queens of Castile and Portugal - is the main Spanish name for the Eurasian magpie (*Pica pica*).

[*Imlac*]

The kindly and avuncular philosopher Imlac appears as a character in Samuel Johnson's *Rasselas*; earlier in the same work (Chapter 6 – 'A dissertation on the art of flying'), Johnson describes an abortive attempt at flight on the part of a 'mechanist' who ends up in a nearby lake, from where Rasselas fetches him, 'half dead with terror and vexation' (ed. J.P. Hardy (OUP, 1988), p. 17).

[*Scenes from the Little Ice Age*]

Galveston: In 1528, Álvar Núñez Cabeza de Vaca and eighty

companions, survivors of the ill-fated Narváez expedition from Cuba to the mainland, were shipwrecked on what is now known as Galveston Island, on the coast of Texas. Rescued (or captured) by local Amerindians, Cabeza de Vaca spent the next eight years among the native peoples of New Spain's outlying regions, establishing himself as a healer and trader, and, with the other three remaining members of the force which had left Cuba -two fellow Spaniards, and an African slave named Estevan – travelling overland through Texas and northern Mexico until they reached Spanish garrisons in Sinaloa, where de Vaca was appalled at the colonizer's treatment of the subject natives.

[*Orpah*]

According to the biblical account, Orpah and Ruth married the sons of Naomi, who had settled in Moab (on the east bank of the Jordan); after the sons die in a famine, Naomi decides to return across the river to Judah, and encourages her daughters-in-law to return to their family homes. Initially they both insist on crossing the Jordan with Naomi, but after she discourages them once more, they come to separate conclusions: 'Orpah kissed her mother-in-law and returned to her people, but Ruth clung to her' (Ruth 1:4

(NEB)); cf. also Laura A. Donaldson, *The Sign of Orpah: Reading Ruth through Native Eyes*, in R.S. Surgirtharajah, ed., *The Postcolonial Biblical Reader* (John Wiley, 2005). Raja Shehadeh mentions fossils discovered in the banks of the Jordan in his *Palestinian Walks: Notes on a Vanishing Landscape* (Profile Books, 2008).

[*Meridian*]

The words in italics are adapted from those of the Lakota holy men Leonard Crow Dog (sections iii & iv) and John Fire Lame Deer (section vi), as recorded by Richard Erdoes, in, respectively, *Crow Dog: Four Generations of Sioux Medicine Men* (New York, NY: HarperCollins, 1995), pp. 44 & 77-8, and *Lame Deer: Seeker of Visions* (Simon & Schuster, 1994/2009), pp. 184-7.

[*Witness*]

The poem draws on the testimony of Tosh Kano, veteran of the Japanese campaigns in South-East Asia, who was stationed in Hiroshima in the summer of 1945, and survived the atomic bombing of the city. Following the establishment of USAAF bases in the Mariana islands, Japanese cities were systematically laid waste in continual bombing raids; until

August, however, only leaflets fell on Hiroshima. The words in italics reproduce the content of one of these, in Kano's translation; cf. Ronald Blythe, ed., *Private Words: Letters and Diaries from the Second World War* (Penguin, 1991), pp. 282-7.

[*Medicine Wheel*]

The Lakota regularly refer to themselves as the *ikche wichasha*, meaning approximately 'ordinary people', 'wild men', or 'real natural human beings'; the *agrapha* are words of Jesus recorded in texts and traditions other than the canonical Gospels.

[*Kidron*]

The list of agricultural products is taken from *Jerusalem in the Time of Jesus*, by Joachim Jeremias (trans. F.H. & C.H. Cave (SCM, 1976), pp. 45-6).